FIGUREHEADS

First published in 2020 by the National Maritime Museum,
Park Row, Greenwich, London SE10 9NF

ISBN: 978-1-906367-63-3

At the heart of the UNESCO World Heritage Site of Maritime
Greenwich are the four world-class attractions of Royal Museums
Greenwich – the National Maritime Museum, the Royal Observatory,
the Queen's House and *Cutty Sark*.

www.rmg.co.uk

Object IDs for all figureheads on page 160

A CIP catalogue record for the book is available from the British Library.

Designed by Ocky Murray
Printed and bound in the UK on FSC certified paper by Gomer Press

FIGUREHEADS

ON THE BOW OF THE SHIP

Sue Prichard

SENIOR CURATOR OF ART

Jeremy Michell

SENIOR CURATOR OF MARITIME TECHNOLOGIES

INTRODUCTION

THE ORIGINS OF THE figurehead lie far back in the pre-historic past. Across the world some cultures decorated their simple vessels with painted eyes to help them 'see' their way safely through the water. This tradition continues today on boats from Malta in the Mediterranean to the Mekong Delta in South East Asia. Carved decoration quickly followed with ancient Egyptian and Greek ships and Viking longboats all possessing recognisable figureheads of varying designs, degrees of sophistication and levels of spiritual meaning.

At its most basic, a 'figurehead' is simply a device at the upper extremity of the stem-post at the bow of the vessel. The initial inspiration for figureheads was, therefore, a mixture of practical decoration to this exposed end of a timber and some form of symbolism, religious or spiritual, to provide protection, ensuring a safe passage for people and goods. However, more robust and varied carvings were added as ship designs changed. The development of larger naval fleets also added a political dimension to these carvings. In the sixteenth and seventeenth centuries, the ships of the

SHIP PLAN FOR *SOVEREIGN OF THE SEAS*, SHOWING FIGUREHEAD DETAIL

Royal Navy became powerful symbols of state and monarch. For example, the elaborate figurehead of the *Sovereign of the Seas*, launched in 1637 as the flagship of Charles I's navy, depicted King Edgar on horseback trampling on crowned figures representing Scotland and Wales. The political nature of naval decoration is best illustrated by the Commonwealth warship *Naseby* (1655), whose figurehead was Oliver Cromwell, also on horseback, suppressing six nations. On Charles II's restoration to the throne in 1660 the ship was renamed the *Royal Charles*, but the image of Cromwell, 'the usurper' and regicide, remained. However, it was later removed and his 'insulting head' was hung from a gibbet on the quayside before being burnt. The diarist and naval administrator Samuel Pepys bemoaned the expense of a replacement: the new figurehead and its associated gilding cost the substantial sum of £51 16s (£5,890).

VIEW FROM THE BOWSPIRIT OF *HERZOGIN CECILE*,
TAKEN BY ALAN VILLIERS, 1929

By the late 1600s, tighter control over naval
expenditure resulted in simpler figureheads for all
warships, except the powerful First Rates, which were
the largest in the fleet. Initially, the typical figurehead
was a stylised full-length lion, but this eventually fell
out of favour by the mid-eighteenth century as other
designs were approved. The later designs included
simple busts and torso carvings of allegorical, classical
and historical figures, animals and birds. The smallest
warships had carved forward or reverse scrolls, known
as billet- and fiddle-heads, at the top of the stem-post.

In contrast to the inspiration for warships, the owners
of merchant ships could choose from a far greater
range of sources. In the case of the record-breaking tea
clipper *Cutty Sark*, Jock Willis chose a carving of the
witch Nannie, who chased Tam o' Shanter in Burns's
poem (see pages 14–17), while other owners selected

figureheads to represent family members, animals or historical, literary and political figures. These carvings were adapted to the size of the ship and, perhaps more importantly, to how much the owner wished to spend: they could be full-, three-quarter-, or merely bust-length, depending on the depth of an owner's pocket. Owners also had the option to buy a generic figurehead. For example, between 1880 and 1920, these were offered by John Roberts from his Port Glasgow workshop at a cost of £3 15s (worth £250 in 1880 and £110 in 1920).

The figurehead embodied the spirit of a ship and was highly symbolic of the personal and collective loyalty of the crew. In *A Smile of Fortune: Harbour Story*, first published in 1912, the author and merchant mariner Joseph Conrad describes a sea captain's indignation at the suggestion he should replace his 'own' figurehead, which had been lost, with a non-specific one from a shipbuilder's yard. In another example, during the Battle of the Glorious First of June in 1794, the hat from the figurehead of the *Brunswick* (74 guns) was shot away. The crew took this as a personal affront. The ship's captain, John Harvey, resolved the situation by offering his own 'superbly laced' hat, which he ordered the carpenter to nail to the bare head of the Duke of Brunswick. In part, this action spurred the crew on to victory over the French, ably demonstrating the importance of the figurehead as the soul of the ship and an inspiration for its company.

Carving figureheads was, of course, a complicated process that required skill, an understanding of wood and an eye for scale, detail and form. By the mid-eighteenth century, the Royal Navy encouraged carvers to submit proposals. Once approved, these were returned, sometimes with alterations, for the carver to begin work. The royal dockyards provided the principal employment opportunities, often for generations of carvers. The Hellyer family, for example, based at Portsmouth and later in London, was particularly prolific. Between 1830 and 1860, they supplied 234 warships with figureheads. The largest, a fearsome Saracen that weighed 2½ tons, was for HMS *Warrior* (1860). Similarly, the Dickerson family, based at Plymouth Dockyard (later Devonport), tendered 33 designs to the Admiralty in the period 1840–60. In 2019, the National Maritime Museum acquired an extensive collection of figurehead and carving designs by the Dickersons, a number of which were submitted to the Admiralty for approval. This new material will further advance our understanding of the history and development these designs.

During the eighteenth and nineteenth centuries, some 150 firms were active in producing ship carvings and while the majority of carvers were men, there is evidence that women were also employed. Abigail and Elizabeth Chichley both worked at Chatham and Sheerness between 1733 and 1777; in 1820 Mrs Lucy Burroughs was employed by Nathaniel Keast at Deptford to supply carvings for HMS *Russell*, HMS *Ariel* and HMS *Southampton*. The Admiralty was prepared to encourage tenders from non-resident carvers if they thought it appropriate and possibly more cost-effective. The wealth of orders generated by the Admiralty has survived in letter books held at the National Archives in Kew, which include over 250 submitted designs. Evidence of this procurement

FIGUREHEADS AT CASTLES' SHIPBREAKING YARD,
BALTIC WHARF, c.1880–1920

process proves that figurehead carving was considered
a professional trade, albeit sometimes combined with
orders for architectural and ecclesiastical carving and
gilding to generate additional income.

When ashore, removed from the ship and divorced
from their original function, an air of the uncanny
surrounds figureheads. They become sources of
inspiration for writers and artists, such as the author
Mrs E. T. Cook, who found the figureheads at the
shipbreaking firm Castles' of Baltic Wharf in London's
Millbank distinctly unsettling and advised 'a strong
mind and a good conscience to travel this way alone
on a dark night'. The self-styled 'Seaside Surrealist'
Eileen Agar was specifically drawn to such curiosities.
During excursions with the artist Paul Nash, she
took several photographs in 1934 of an abandoned
female half-figure juxtaposed with a ship's wheel.
The figurehead still resides in the same place at

Falmouth. In the eighteenth century, satirical artists used the figurehead as anti-French propaganda. In *The Humours of an Election* (1755), William Hogarth depicts Tory and Whig agents attempting to bribe an innkeeper for his vote. Two old sailors re-enact a battle using broken clay pipes to the right of the image, while outside the door to the inn on the left is a large and startlingly demonic red lion figurehead devouring a French fleur-de-lis. More recently, where figureheads survive in museums outside a maritime context they have been appropriated as 'folk art', a term used to describe a variety of handmade objects produced by untrained amateurs using traditional techniques. In *English Popular Art* (1951), the folk art collectors Enid Marx and Margaret Lambert noted that 'carvings on ships, especially the figureheads, is one of the most characteristic expressions of popular art in a seafaring nation'. They also connected the demise of the figurehead with emergence of the mid-Victorian vogue for gaudy fairground carousel animals and rocking horses. In fact, some carvers, such as John Robert Anderson of Bristol, subsequently became famous for ornamental fairground work.

Figurehead survival owes much to their emotional resonance, a ghostly reminder of a once proud warship or trading vessel and those who sailed in them. Some are the only existing reminder, acting as unofficial memorials to lives lost. The 'Valhalla' collection on Tresco, for instance, consists of around 30 mostly merchant figureheads and carvings commemorating the nineteenth-century sailing vessels and early steamships wrecked off the Isles of Scilly. Similarly, in the graveyard at Morwenstow, north Cornwall, a

figurehead of a female Highland warrior marks the graves of those lost on the brig *Caledonia*, wrecked in 1842. Recognised for its cultural significance, a modern replica replaced the original, which was restored in 2004 and placed in the church.

Until the middle of the twentieth century, small collections of ship figureheads were often found in shipbreakers' yards. As early as 1860, a visitor to the impressive figurehead display at Castles' of Millbank acknowledged their aesthetic value, noting they were 'more or less artistically carved and therefore worth preserving'. Sadly, Castles', originally founded in 1838, was destroyed by bombing in 1941 during the London Blitz. However, a small display of figureheads returned to Millbank for Tate Britain's 'British Folk Art' exhibition in 2014.

PART OF THE FIGUREHEAD COLLECTION AT *CUTTY SARK*, GREENWICH

The transition from ship fixture to folk art, from sea to land, has ensured that figureheads continue to inspire and intrigue. Variously a memorial, souvenir, garden ornament or curiosity, fundamentally figureheads belong to the seafarer, as recognised by the naval officer and poet Captain Ronald Hopwood:

You may search the North Seas over
till you find the British Fleet,
And at first, perhaps, you'll think
that figureheads are obsolete;
But the sailor-folk can see them
where they always used to be,
Full of strength and mystic meaning,
gazing far and out to sea!

'The Figureheads',
from *The Old Way and Other Poems* (1916)

FIGUREHEADS AT THE NATIONAL MARITIME MUSEUM AND *CUTTY SARK*

THE NATIONAL MARITIME MUSEUM is home to one of the most extensive collections of ship figureheads in the world. Numbering nearly 100, it includes many British naval carvings illustrating the vast array of inspirational subject matter used during the eighteenth and nineteenth centuries. The collection includes large full-length figures of classical and allegorical heroes, busts of historical figures and a wide range of realistic or stylised animals and birds. The majority of the collection came from Devonport Dockyard in 1936–37 with others acquired from the old Royal United Services Institution Museum, the Chatham and Woolwich Royal Dockyards and the Royal Navy training establishment HMS *Ganges*.

In addition, the historic sailing ship *Cutty Sark* (1869), which along with the National Maritime Museum is part of Royal Museums Greenwich, displays a unique collection of 80 merchant ship figureheads assembled by Sydney Cumbers, a private collector affectionately known as 'Long John Silver'. Cumbers dedicated the collection to all who served in the Merchant Navy and sailed in the fleet of Dunkirk Little Ships during Operation Dynamo in May 1940. Together these two important collections of extraordinary figureheads, often the only tangible surviving evidence of a sailing or steam ship, are among the star attractions in the Museum's vast holdings of maritime history.

NANNIE

VESSEL: *CUTTY SARK*

DATE OF VESSEL: 1869

VESSEL TYPE: TEA CLIPPER

FIGUREHEAD HEIGHT: 2.4 M

NANNIE DEE IS A fictional character in Robert Burns's epic poem 'Tam o' Shanter' (1790–91). Presented as both a lurid ghost story and a warning against the perils of alcohol, the poem follows the misfortune of the drunken Tam. Ignoring the advice of his comely wife at home, Tam stays out too late and stumbles upon a coven of warlocks and witches engaged in a satanic dance. Entranced by the eroticism of the beautiful witch Nannie in her short linen shift, or cutty sark, Tam exclaims 'Weel done, Cutty-sark!' Alerted to his presence, the 'hellish legion' give chase. Tam manages to escape Nannie's vengeful wrath, although his mare, Maggie, is less fortunate – the witch grabs hold of her tail, leaving poor Maggie 'with scarce a stump'.

Witchcraft and other pagan rituals were practised in England and Scotland for centuries. However, during the reigns of Elizabeth I and James VI witches were increasingly seen as a danger to society. James VI's philosophical dissertation *Daemonologie* (1597) sought to justify the persecution of witches. Shakespeare may have been inspired by *Daemonologie* to create the witches in *Macbeth*. 'Witch-hunting' reached its peak in the seventeenth century, but did not cease until the Witchcraft Act of 1735, which

Burns's narrative poem transforms the beautiful Nannie into a popular male sexual fantasy

abolished this ruthless oppression. Written over 50 years after the Act, Burns's narrative poem against the perils of witchcraft and women transforms the beautiful Nannie into a popular male sexual fantasy rather than a threatening demonic force.

Burns has been described as a 'radical libertarian, who was ... sceptical of the usual socially-constructed assumptions about gender in the 18th century'. By the middle of the nineteenth century, these assumptions were popularised in Victorian art and literature, most notably in the English poet Coventry Patmore's ode to his wife, 'The Angel in the House' (1854). Patmore's central female character is modest, chaste and innocent, submissively supporting her husband. The character of Nannie Dee overtly challenges this ideal stereotype. Her provocative dancing, in which she flaunts her sexuality, deviates from the prevailing social norms. In Victorian terms, she is thus a 'fallen woman', challenging middle-class men's moral authority.

Within the context of mid-Victorian morality, Nannie Dee is a curious choice for a ship figurehead. Sailors were notoriously superstitious, believing that women on board would bring bad luck. Moreover, in British folklore, witches were able to conjure up storms at sea and sink ships. In sharp contrast to *Cutty Sark*, witches were also physically unable to cross water, as described in Burns's poem: 'A running stream they dare na cross'. Socially, the Victorian merchant represented the epitome of respectability. He was the ideal husband and father, providing financial security for his family. As a proud Scot, John 'Jock' Willis's roots played an important role in the identity of the family's shipping business. Many of their ships were named after Scottish places and rivers, but *Cutty Sark* was unusual being the only Willis ship with a literary name. As an unmarried man, Jock may have appreciated the humour in Burns's ironic warning against alcohol and women, and relished the joke in naming the tea clipper after Nannie's nickname.

Frederick Hellyer carved the original Nannie figurehead, which was removed during restoration and replaced in 1955 by a new version by Arthur Levison. Another substitute was commissioned in 2018, whose design more closely matches the original.

PERSONIFICATION OF THE RIVER DEE

VESSEL: HMS *DEE*

DATE OF VESSEL: 1832

VESSEL TYPE: 6-GUN WOODEN PADDLE WARSHIP, LATER A TROOPSHIP THEN A STORE SHIP

FIGUREHEAD HEIGHT: 1.4 M

A HALF-LENGTH FIGUREHEAD of a bearded and crowned river god representing the River Dee in north-west England, an important area for shipbuilding. In Greek and Roman iconography, river gods were visually associated with Poseidon/Neptune, the ruler of the seas. For example, early-nineteenth-century statues representing the Tiber and the Nile both depict bearded gods with relevant attributes like an oar for navigation or a cornucopia for wealth and trade. In the case of HMS *Dee* these symbols may have been on the trail-board down each side of the supporting stem-post. Naming Royal Navy warships after British rivers continues to this day.

GIUSEPPI GARIBALDI

VESSEL: *GARIBALDI*

DATE OF VESSEL: UNKNOWN

VESSEL TYPE: MERCHANT SHIP

FIGUREHEAD HEIGHT: 1.5 M

AS ONE OF THE founding fathers of a united Italy, Giuseppi Garibaldi (1807–82) was famous in his day as a revolutionary and nationalist. In 1864, he was enthusiastically received during a visit to Britain as a liberator and Italian hero. This encouraged the commercial production of commemorative merchandise, such as plates, cups and figurines. This almost full-length figurehead shows him in a light blue jacket with red necktie loosely around his neck. In his left hand is a scroll. Garibaldi is depicted with his famous full beard and long hair curled at the neck, looking the part of an idealistic nation-builder.

ATALANTA,
GREEK HUNTRESS

VESSEL: HMS *ATALANTA*

DATE OF VESSEL: 1847

VESSEL TYPE: 16-GUN WOODEN BRIG

FIGUREHEAD HEIGHT: 1.7 M

A THREE-QUARTER-LENGTH female figurehead of the mythical Greek huntress Atalanta. She was famed for running swiftly and refused to marry unless a suitor could first defeat her in a race. During one contest, Milanion dropped three golden apples, a gift from Venus, which Atalanta stopped to collect, allowing him to win the race. The figurehead depicts Atalanta in a green, loose-flowing dress that has slipped from her left shoulder. The trail-board below her dress has a bow and arrow carved into it, picked out in red and gold paint, reinforcing her status as a hunter.

EAGLE

VESSEL: UNKNOWN

DATE OF VESSEL: UNKNOWN

VESSEL TYPE: MERCHANT SHIP

FIGUREHEAD HEIGHT: 1.5 M

THIS FIGUREHEAD SHOWS an eagle, its wings outstretched, standing on the scroll of the stem-post. The origin of the figurehead is uncertain, but it may be American as there is the possibility that the ship was built there. The type of eagle is not identifiable – none have the feather 'ruff' around the neck – but it is emblematic of the United States, where the bald eagle is the national bird. It also appears on the nation's Great Seal, grasping thirteen arrows representing the founding states of the Union – in its left talon and an olive branch of peace in its right.

FREDERICK WILLIAM III, KING OF PRUSSIA

VESSEL: HMS *FREDERICK WILLIAM*

DATE OF VESSEL: 1860

VESSEL TYPE: 86-GUN AUXILIARY FIRST RATE WARSHIP

FIGUREHEAD HEIGHT: 2.7 M

THIS FIGUREHEAD REPRESENTS King Frederick William III of Prussia (1770–1840). The name *Royal Frederick* was allocated to a 110-gun warship, but when finally launched as an 86-gun steam warship, it was renamed *Frederick William*. The figurehead is based on contemporary illustrations and shows the king wearing a high-collared, blue uniform with red sash and epaulettes, but these may not be the original colours. Frederick William's forces played a significant role in the Napoleonic Wars. Although initially defeated by France, the Prussian army proved vital in defeating Napoleon in 1813–14 and again at Waterloo in June 1815 when its timely arrival secured victory for the allies.

GAIUS MARCIUS CORIOLANUS

VESSEL: *CORIOLANUS*

DATE OF VESSEL: 1876

VESSEL TYPE: THREE-MASTED MERCHANT SHIP

FIGUREHEAD HEIGHT: 1.3 M

THREE-QUARTER-LENGTH bust of the Roman general Gaius Marcius Coriolanus, who was reputedly a war hero turned traitor when he joined forces with an enemy of Rome in around 490 BC. However, he is better known as the tragic central character in Shakespeare's tragedy *Coriolanus* and it is likely that this fictionalised version is the inspiration for the vessel's name. The figurehead shows him in stylised Roman chainmail armour and a helmet with cheek guards. It is a replacement, carved in 1902, after the original full-length figurehead was lost when *Coriolanus* ran aground during a hurricane in Algoa Bay, South Africa.

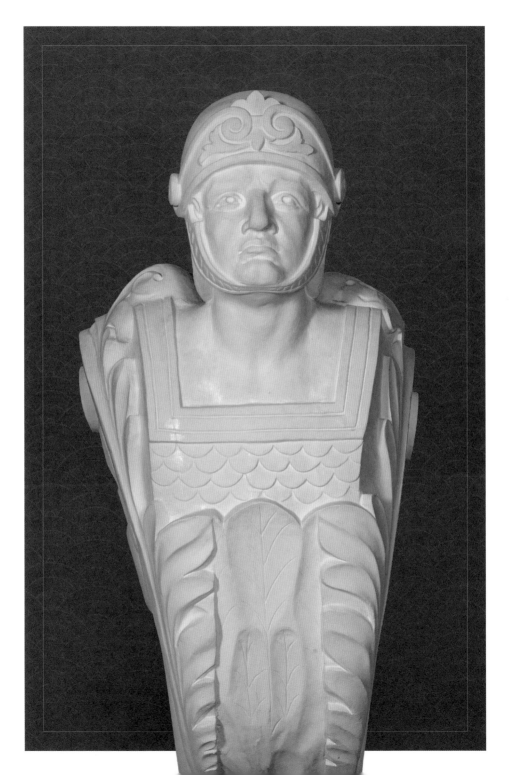

UNKNOWN FEMALE FIGURE

VESSEL: UNKNOWN

DATE OF VESSEL: UNKNOWN

VESSEL TYPE: UNKNOWN FRENCH MERCHANT SHIP

FIGUREHEAD HEIGHT: 1.9 M

IT IS BELIEVED THIS figurehead comes from a French merchantman wrecked off the Cornish coast. The three-quarter-length female figure holds a posy, with a closed fan held across the body in her left hand. In terms of dress, the neckline, sleeve flounces and floral corsage reflect court fashions of the late 1750s. The tightly curled hairstyle, known as *tête de mouton* (literally 'sheep's head'), remained popular until the 1760s, being associated with Maria Josepha of Saxony, the devoted wife of Louis de France, the eldest son of King Louis XV. It is likely that this nineteenth-century merchant figurehead represents her.

LEDA, WIFE OF KING TYNDARUS OF SPARTA

VESSEL: HMS *LEDA*

DATE OF VESSEL: 1828

VESSEL TYPE: 46-GUN FIFTH RATE FRIGATE

FIGUREHEAD HEIGHT: 1.6 M

LEDA WAS THE WIFE of the Spartan King Tyndarus. While bathing, she was raped by Zeus in the guise of a swan. In some versions of the myth, which vary considerably in detail, she laid two eggs each producing twins: the warriors Castor and Pollux, and the beauties Helen of Troy and Clytemnestra. The bust-length figurehead does not show her with a swan, although it may have been represented on the trailboard below. Leda is wearing a simple shirt with what may be a version of a Greek peplos mantle draped over it, pinned at each shoulder with large brooches.

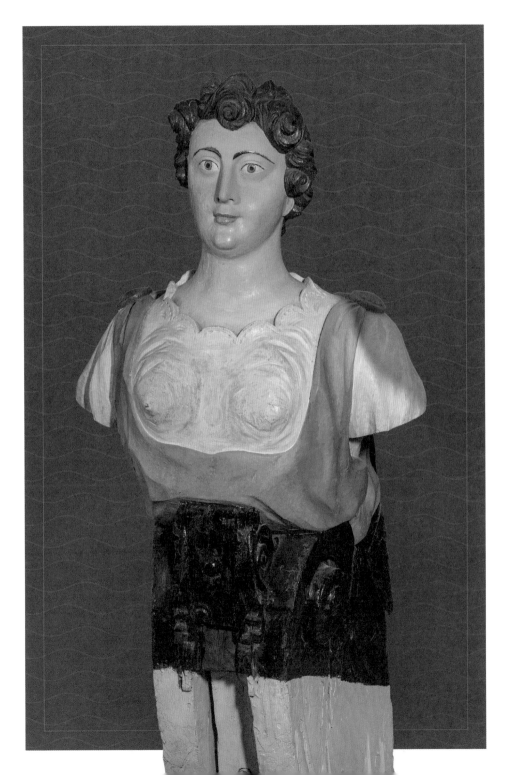

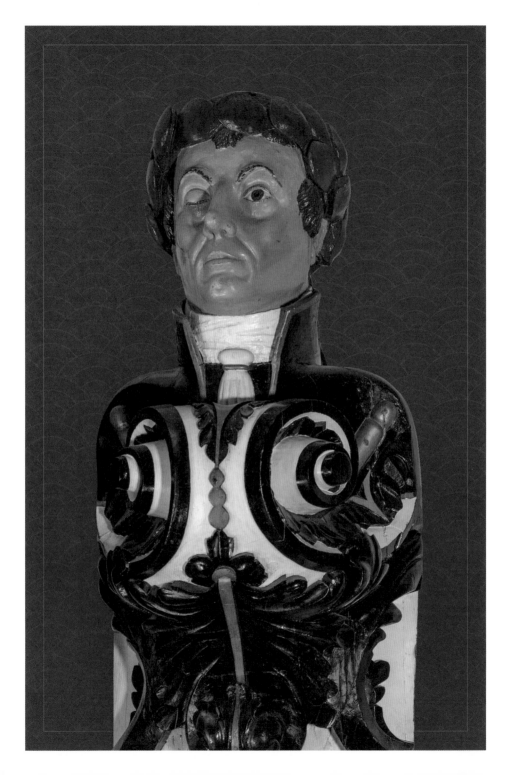

VICE-ADMIRAL LORD NELSON

VESSEL: HMS *HORATIO*

DATE OF VESSEL: 1807

VESSEL TYPE: 38-GUN FIFTH RATE FRIGATE

FIGUREHEAD HEIGHT: 1.7 M

HMS *HORATIO* WAS the first warship to commemorate Nelson (1758–1805) and the figurehead is a bust-length representation. Rather than use one of the many images of him in naval uniform, he is shown in civilian clothes: a high-collared coat and white cravat. However, harking back to ancient Rome, he wears a laurel crown representing his victories. The closed eyelid alludes to Nelson's loss of effective sight in his right eye in 1794, meaning he could only distinguish light and shade. A stylised marshal's baton rests against the right shoulder, partially obscured by the fiddle-head scrollwork that dominates the lower part of the carving.

HARLEQUIN

VESSEL: HMS *HARLEQUIN*

DATE OF VESSEL: 1836

VESSEL TYPE: 16-GUN WOODEN SECOND CLASS BRIG

FIGUREHEAD HEIGHT: 1.5 M

ROBERT HALL OF LONDON, who provided 21 figureheads for the Royal Navy between 1832 and 1837, carved the original figurehead. In 1845, when Harlequin was under repair at Portsmouth Dockyard, Hellyer submitted a design for a replacement bust at an estimated cost of £6 15s (around £460 today). This figurehead is close to the original design, suggesting the Navy requested few alterations. Hellyer added a cloak, here painted blue, resting on the scroll-head. The ship was converted to a coal hulk in 1860 and sold in 1889 to Marshall of Plymouth for breaking. The nimble and distinctively clad Harlequin was a popular slapstick pantomime character in the early nineteenth century, imported from the seventeenth-century Italian *Commedia del Art* tradition.

AJAX

VESSEL: *AJAX*

DATE OF VESSEL: 1846

VESSEL TYPE: 74-GUN THIRD RATE CONVERTED TO AUXILIARY SCREW SHIP

FIGUREHEAD HEIGHT: 4.5 M

CLASSICAL WARRIORS WERE popular subjects for figureheads. In Homer's epic Greek poem, *The Iliad*, Ajax the Great was the son of King Telamon, one of Jason's famous Argonauts. Described as a man of great stature, colossal frame and the strongest of all the Achaeans, Ajax was capable of holding off the enemy single-handedly. This towering figurehead, the largest in the Museum's collection, illustrates the key attributes of the great warrior and epitomises virile masculinity. The Greeks considered the human form the most important subject in the hierarchy of artistic genres. The earliest and possibly most famous depiction of Ajax is the Belvedere Torso in the Museo Pio-Clementio, of the Vatican Museums, a monumental marble sculpture carved in the first century BC which represents the physical perfection of Ajax in early maturity.

The latter half of the eighteenth century witnessed a shift in topical debate regarding differing ideals of manliness. The 'fop', or 'macaroni', was replaced by a different type of gentleman, relying less on superfluous adornment and more on sartorial restraint, heightened physicality and strength of character. As a microcosm of wider society, the Royal Navy shaped the masculine identities of both officers and men. Within this context Ajax represents an amalgamation of Greek principles of harmony and order with stereotypical tropes of naval manliness, bravery, stoicism and self-sacrifice – all deemed supremely British characteristics. The figurehead is further identified with such attributes by the addition of a British order of chivalry. From the 1770s, the Order of the Bath was awarded to naval and military personnel as well as to

The great warrior also functions as a warning of the danger of hubris or arrogance

politicians and diplomats. Appropriating a mythological Greek hero into contemporary British naval culture thus creates a role model for the ship's company. Officers and seamen could aspire to feats of great courage during combat, creating their own personal mythology surrounding acts of heroism.

In addition to serving as an inspirational role model, the great warrior also functions as a warning of the danger of hubris or arrogance. Following the death of Achilles, Ajax and his comrade-in-arms Odysseus both claim the magical armour of the fallen warrior. A competition is held, which Odysseus wins with the help of the goddess Athena. Demented with rage, and further tricked by Athena, Ajax slaughters herds of livestock, believing them to be his enemies. Reeling from his failure, and now conscious of the enormity of this unwarranted carnage, Ajax is unable to live with his shame and falls upon his own sword. Ajax's decline and disgrace acted as a warning against rash behaviour. While orders and decisions may be unfair, ultimately authority must be preserved and good conduct maintained through self-control.

The mythological hero embodies both honour and sacrifice

For the crew of *Ajax*, the figurehead represents more than simply an ornamental feature of ship decoration. The mythological hero embodies both honour and sacrifice, his story told and retold as a potent narrative within the close community at sea. Set within the crowded, highly charged, single-sex world of a warship, this particular example may also reflect potential sexual desire. Certainly to modern eyes, the idealised physique of Ajax, with his full, sensuous lips, exposed muscular torso and extravagant plumed helmet could be regarded as an objective focus for necessarily repressed homoerotic fantasies.

HIAWATHA

VESSEL: *HIAWATHA*

DATE OF VESSEL: 1891

VESSEL TYPE: THREE-MASTED STEEL SAILING SHIP

FIGUREHEAD HEIGHT: 2.3 M

HIAWATHA WAS A FIRST NATIONS leader who, together with the Prophet Deganawida (The Great Peacemaker), co-founded the Iroquois confederacy of Five Nations comprising the Mohawk, Onongade, Oneida, Cayuga and Senaca tribes. Hiawatha's exact dates are unknown but it is believed he lived between 1525 and 1595. A skilled orator, Hiawatha's teachings on peace and forgiveness were passed down through oral tradition and are still in use today.

The character of Hiawatha is best known as the hero of Henry Wadsworth Longfellow's epic poem *The Song of Hiawatha* (1855). A composite of various narratives and accounts by contemporary ethnographers, the poem tells the tragic, but fictional,

story of the legendary peacemaker Hiawatha and his beautiful female lover, Minnehaha. It received international acclaim and helped solidify the concept of a pre-contact race whose fate was sealed by exposure to the supposedly civilising influence of the West. Since its publication, *The Song of Hiawatha* has been translated into more than 45 languages.

Longfellow's treatment of Hiawatha, and his idealisation of the Native American as 'the noble savage' is emblematic of eighteenth- and nineteenth-

> *The poem tells the tragic, but fictional, story of the legendary peacemaker Hiawatha and his beautiful female lover*

century representations of 'the other' in the art and literature of the period. For instance, American writers drew on First Nation oral tradition to construct an 'authentic' literary tradition based on these ideals. Longfellow drew heavily on the ethnographer Henry Rowe Schoolcraft's *Algic Researches* (1839), who translated into English the oral histories of his wife's Chippewa heritage. In creating his hero, Longfellow substituted the Chippewa name Manabozho for the more palatable, but Iroquoian, Hiawatha. Such sentimentalism generated severe criticism among those who believed in a predominantly white, male, western supremacy. One reviewer of *The Song of Hiawatha* expressed 'regret that our own pet national poet should not have selected as the theme of his muse something higher and better than the silly legend of the savage aborigines'.

The figurehead of Hiawatha can be read as the stereotype of a recognisable Indian character translated into a romantic ideal, the hero of 'an idealized tableau of American life long ago, far long ago, before the Machine's reign'. The 1,498-ton merchant ship *Hiawatha* was built in 1891 for H. Bjorn Jnr of Kragero, Norway. Mass emigration from rural Norway to North America reached its peak in the nineteenth century and accounts of Native Americans appear in travel literature, guidebooks and letters. These narratives often draw on prevailing stereotypes, presenting Native Americans as either savages or harmless primitives. The 'Pipe of Peace'

> *Prevailing stereotypes presenting Native Americans as either savages or harmless primitives*

held in Hiawatha's right hand suggests a more positive depiction, the drawing together of nations under the constitution known as 'The Great Law of Peace'.

In 1917 Bjorn sold *Hiawatha* to a Mr Hansen who named the ship *Fiskjo*. It was sold to the Dover Shipbreaking Company in 1924. The large full-length figurehead was found by Sydney 'Long John Silver' Cumbers in a garden at Kearney, near Dover, and presented to the Cutty Sark Preservation Society in 1953.

PERSONIFICATION OF A NAVAL BATTLE

VESSEL: *NAVARINO*

DATE OF VESSEL: UNKNOWN

VESSEL TYPE: MERCHANT SHIP

FIGUREHEAD HEIGHT: 0.8 M

THIS HALF-LENGTH FEMALE figurehead in a blue-green dress with detail and gold buttons was located on the Queen's Head Hotel, Ramsgate. It is thought to come from a trading brig wrecked at Pegwell while trying to enter Ramsgate Harbour. The name Navarino possibly relates to the battle fought between the allied navies of Britain, France and Russia against the Ottoman and Egyptian fleet in 1827. This was the last major battle the Royal Navy fought with an all-sail fleet. As the nineteenth century progressed, warships were fitted with auxiliary steam power and, later, masts were removed altogether.

PRESIDENT ABRAHAM LINCOLN

VESSEL: *ABRAHAM LINCOLN*	
DATE OF VESSEL: UNKNOWN	
VESSEL TYPE: MERCHANT SHIP	
FIGUREHEAD HEIGHT: 1.4 M	

ABRAHAM LINCOLN'S (1809–65) characteristic hair and beard have been captured by the carver, making him easily recognisable. The figurehead reflects photographs of him in formal attire with a waistcoat and bowtie, although the coat, normally open, has been buttoned up and his right hand is placed between the flaps. Lincoln was the sixteenth President of the United States and in office during the American Civil War, achieving victory for the Union. He famously abolished slavery with the Thirteenth Amendment. Lincoln was shot by an aggrieved Confederate, John Wilkes Booth, at the theatre on 14 April 1865. He died the following day.

GANNET

VESSEL: HMS *GANNET*

DATE OF VESSEL: 1857

VESSEL TYPE: 11-GUN WOODEN SCREW SLOOP

FIGUREHEAD HEIGHT: 1.6 M

IT WAS COMMON FOR smaller warships named after animals to have it depicted as the figurehead. The alternative was a representation in human form, such as Hellyer's proposed options for HMS *Cormorant* (1842) of a Chinese fisherman, who traditionally use tame cormorants to catch fish. For HMS *Gannet*, the Dickersons carved the bird with its wings folded, standing on the billet-head of the stem-post, as if waiting to dive into the water to catch fish. This is a simple figurehead, but the bird's characteristics as a voracious hunter were perfect for the political statement it was making.

WILLIAM PITT THE YOUNGER

VESSEL: *WILLIAM PITT*

DATE OF VESSEL: UNKNOWN

VESSEL TYPE: MERCHANT SHIP

FIGUREHEAD HEIGHT: 0.6 M

WHEN APPOINTED IN 1783, William Pitt the Younger (1759–1806) became Britain's youngest Prime Minister aged only 24. He was in post until 1801 and again from 1804 to his death in 1806. He dominated politics during a series of national crises, including the end of the War of American Independence, the French Revolutionary and Napoleonic Wars, and the constitutional pressures of George III's illness. Tens of thousands of mourners passed his coffin when he lay in state, emphasising Pitt's popularity. Rather appropriately for a figurehead, he became a symbol of duty and dedication against sometimes impossible odds.

FIGURE HEAD
OF
H.M.S. "THAMES".

FATHER THAMES

VESSEL: HMS *THAMES*

DATE OF VESSEL: 1823

VESSEL TYPE: 46-GUN FIFTH RATE FRIGATE

FIGUREHEAD HEIGHT: 0.9 M

THIS FIGUREHEAD THAT once adorned a 46-gun frigate depicts Old Father Thames, the personification of the river. The expressive figurehead has been carved in a High-Baroque style with the statues of Renaissance Rome in mind. The Thames was, of course, an important river, being the main trading route into London and the world's busiest port until the mid-twentieth century. It was also a significant shipbuilding centre with royal dockyards and numerous private firms. In the nineteenth century, before proper sanitation was introduced, cartoonists in magazines like *Punch* used the figure of Father Thames to highlight the polluted state of the river.

ALECTO,
A GREEK FURY

VESSEL: HMS *IMPLACABLE*

DATE OF VESSEL: CAPTURED 1805

VESSEL TYPE: 74-GUN THIRD RATE, TWO-DECKER WARSHIP

FIGUREHEAD HEIGHT: 2.3 M

PREVIOUSLY ASSUMED TO represent the Gorgon Medusa, this is actually one of the three Furies of Greek and Roman legend. The Furies, goddesses of vengeance, pursued and punished wrongdoers. The change in name to *Implacable* indicates that this is the Fury Alecto ('she who rests not'). As a political comment, the figurehead also has a fleur-de-lys in a central position below the main bust. This was the emblem of the French Bourbon monarchy and is more a statement of British solidarity with the Bourbon cause during the Napoleonic Wars than a piece of one-upmanship for having captured a French warship.

BRITISH NAVAL SEAMAN

VESSEL: HMS *DARING*

DATE OF VESSEL: 1844

VESSEL TYPE: 12-GUN WOODEN SAILING BRIG

FIGUREHEAD HEIGHT: 0.9 M

BUST-LENGTH FIGUREHEAD of a male sailor in 'square rig'. This uniform was formally introduced for naval ratings in 1857, although it was in unofficial use earlier. This style of uniform, with its three white stripes on the wide navy blue collar and black silk, is still used on ceremonial occasions. The badge on his left arm indicates that he is a Petty Officer. The sailor is also wearing the sennet (straw) hat with 'Daring' on the cap tally. The original sketch for this figurehead shows an informal outfit, suggesting that the post-1857 colours were painted later to reflect the uniform change.

PERSONIFICATION OF THE CITY OF LONDON

VESSEL: HMS *LONDON*

DATE OF VESSEL: 1840

VESSEL TYPE: 90-GUN SECOND RATE, TWO-DECKER

FIGUREHEAD HEIGHT: 2.1 M

FIGUREHEADS WERE ALSO created for warships named after British cities, a long-standing Royal Navy tradition. In this case London is represented by a woman wearing a mural crown. The crown is likely to be based on the White Tower at the Tower of London. Not all figureheads survived through a ship's entire career and this one was removed when HMS *London* was converted to a steam warship in 1857/58. A new figurehead, more elegant than this one, was added. However, the original version survived, being stored, like many other figureheads, at Devonport until transfer to the Museum in 1937.

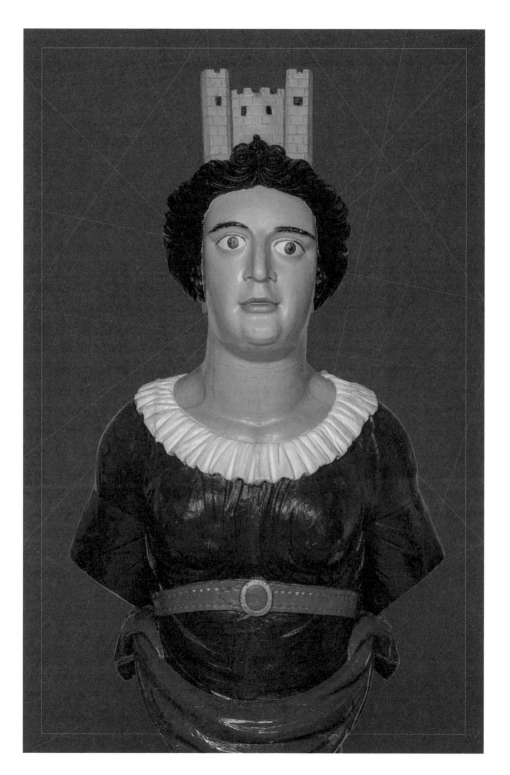

NIKE, GREEK GODDESS OF VICTORY

VESSEL:	*VICTORY*
DATE OF VESSEL:	1805
VESSEL TYPE:	FUNERAL CAR
FIGUREHEAD HEIGHT:	1 M

THIS IS NOT STRICTLY a ship's figurehead, as it was mounted on the front of Lord Nelson's funeral car that took his body to St Paul's Cathedral on 9 January 1806. It represents the mythical Greek messenger Nike (goddess of Victory), a direct link to HMS *Victory* (1765) and the naval victory at Trafalgar. The *Morning Post* of 8 January 1806 described the funeral car as 'decorated with Escutchions, Bannerolls and Emblematical devices'. She holds a victor's laurel wreath in her raised right hand and a palm frond in her left, which was carried in ancient Roman triumphal processions after a great victory.

OMAR PASHA LATAS

VESSEL: *OMAR PASHA*

DATE OF VESSEL: UNKNOWN

VESSEL TYPE: MERCHANT SHIP

FIGUREHEAD HEIGHT: 0.8 M

OMAR PASHA (1806–71) was born into a Christian family in Croatia when it was part of the Austrian Empire. He later converted to Islam and changed his name to Omar Pasha after escaping when his father was convicted of misappropriation. He was a very successful and well-regarded general in the Ottoman army, having fought against the Russians during the Crimean War (1853–56) alongside the French and British armies. This three-quarter-length figurehead shows him in his prime, decorated with a large number of medals, including a version of the Order of Medjidie suspended below his neck stock.

SARACEN WARRIOR

VESSEL: HMS *HIMALAYA*

DATE OF VESSEL: 1854

VESSEL TYPE: IRON STEAM SCREW TROOPSHIP

FIGUREHEAD HEIGHT: 2.5 M

THE *HIMALAYA* WAS built for P&O in 1853 at C.J. Mare and Co. of Blackwall. At 3,553 tons, it was one of the largest passenger ships of the mid-nineteenth century. It was purchased by the Admiralty in 1854, becoming HMS *Himalaya*, and used as a troopship until 1894. During active service, the *Himalaya* carried up to 3,000 troops to India, South Africa, the Gold Coast and North America. It supported operations in the Second Opium War (1856–60).

The three-quarter-length male figurehead is wearing a traditional Muslim headdress consisting of a long scarf wound around a small cap and dressed in a fighting tunic. He is armed with a short sword, or scimitar, traditionally associated with the East. The decorative motifs on the tunic suggests a rudimentary attempt at Islamic calligraphy.

Early historians and Christian theologians ascribe the term Saracen, or *Saraceni*, to a particular ethnic group located in the Hejaxi region of the Arabian Peninsular, north of the Islamic holy city of Medina. However, 'Saracen' was later used as a derogatory term by the Roman and Byzantine Empires to describe any Arabian Muslim. Ninth-century chronicles describe 'Saracen' raiders carrying out pirate attacks throughout the Mediterranean, conquering Malta, Sicily, Crete, the Italian mainland and the South of France. It is likely that these raids were part of a well-coordinated naval campaign to open up highly profitable trade routes.

> *'Saracen' was used as a derogatory term by the Roman and Byzantine Empires to describe any Arabian Muslim*

In the second half of the nineteenth century, especially after the 1857–58 mutiny and rebellion in India, the British began to construct the idea of 'martial races', peoples whose warlike attitudes were tempered by loyalty. For example, Highland Scots, Sikhs and Nepalese Gurkhas were all deemed 'martial' and capable of forming reliable regiments in the cause of empire. Often from mountainous regions, they were deemed to be naturally tough and devoid of the worldly outlook that might encourage questioning and insubordination. The image of the mighty Saracen and the name *Himalaya*, therefore, perfectly embody the pseudo-theory of a 'martial race', which was, of course, wholly appropriate for a troopship.

'The Saracen's Head' was a popular name for pubs and inns, with the earliest dating to the sixteenth century

'The Saracen's Head' was also a popular name for pubs and inns, with some of the earliest dating to the sixteenth century. According to local legend 'The Saracen's Head' or 'Ye Royal Saracens Hedde' in Beaconsfield was named by Richard I, who stayed at the inn on his return from the Crusades. While no longer commonplace, painted pub signs featuring a generic portrait of a bearded man wearing a traditional Muslim headdress can still be found in coastal and rural locations.

LALLA ROOKH

VESSEL: *LALLA ROOKH*	
DATE OF VESSEL: 1856	
VESSEL TYPE: WOODEN CLIPPER	
FIGUREHEAD HEIGHT: 2.1 M	

LALLA ROOKH, FROM the Persian meaning 'tulip cheeked', was the title character in a book-length romantic poem by Thomas Moore, published in 1817. It tells the story of the princess's journey from Delhi to Kashmir to marry a prince she had never met. On the journey she was entertained by an unknown poet, who turned out to be the prince in disguise. The use of literary characters as inspiration for naming ships was fairly common. Other literary figureheads in the Museum's collection include Sir Lancelot, made famous by Sir Thomas Mallory's book *Mort D'Arthur* about King Arthur, Friar Tuck from the legends about Robin Hood, and Hiawatha, who was immortalised in Henry Longfellow's 1855 epic poem *Song of Hiawatha*.

The use of exotic settings and themes in art and literature was popular in the nineteenth century, inspired by a wave of interest in the culture, religion, art, languages and philosophies of Asia. This broader intellectual and artistic awareness of the 'Orient' (a medieval term) became known as 'Orientalism'. Interest in India was further heightened during the Great Exhibition of 1851, where a dizzying array of goods and artefacts from the sub-continent dominated the space allocated for 'imperial' displays at the very heart of the Crystal Palace, sparking extensive newspaper coverage.

The figurehead may have been inspired by the original illustrations from the published poem with common, if stylised, features. These include long, flowing locks,

The use of exotic settings and themes in art and literature was popular in the nineteenth century

the tasselled cord that has been adapted into the edge tassel of her jacket, and the headdress, consisting of a jewelled headband and a diaphanous silk veil swept back over her hair.

Older photographs of the figurehead show that the paint scheme was a rich dark one of green, red and gold, illustrating that over time figureheads can lose their original colour schemes. Closer inspection of the figurehead shows that there is a hollow tube running from the lamp down her arm and under her armpit. This suggests that at some point the lamp was designed to be used with oil, perhaps on windless days in harbour as a novelty stunt or, more likely, adapted after the figurehead was brought ashore.

> *The lamp was designed to be used with oil, perhaps on windless days in harbour as a novelty stunt*

Either way, the lamp links back to the poem, where the final stanzas are entitled 'The Light of the Haram', a metaphor for the beauty of one of the women who lived in the harem and for Kashmir. The figurehead takes this idea and suggests that the new beauty will be Lalla Rookh, as she is now holding the lamp.

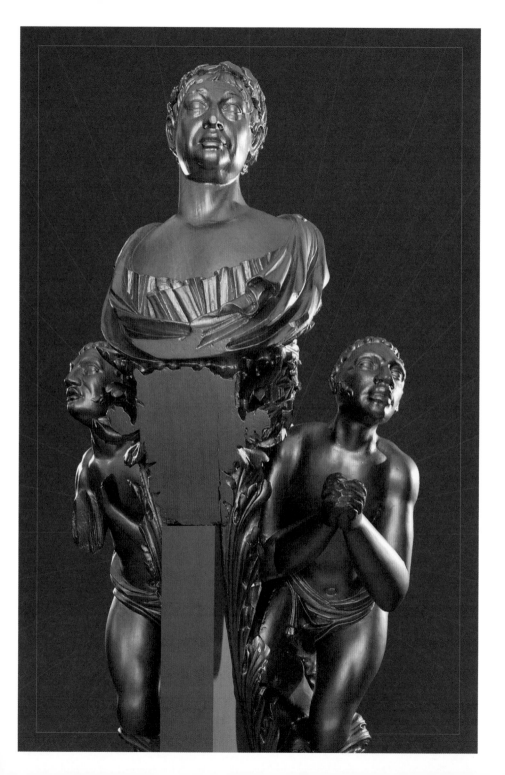

KING GEORGE III

VESSEL: *ROYAL GEORGE*	
DATE OF VESSEL: 1817	
VESSEL TYPE: ROYAL YACHT	
FIGUREHEAD HEIGHT: 1.9 M	

A GOLD-PAINTED FIGUREHEAD in the form of a classical-style bust of George III (1738–1820) wearing the laurel wreath of a victor. Either side is a supplicating African supporter with arms raised in front. While the interpretation of the figurehead is not clear, there are a couple of possible ideas. The first is that the supporters relate to the famous Wedgwood's 'Am I not a man and a brother?' plaque, produced as part of the campaign to abolish the slave trade. However, while the iconography is similar, the other suggestion is that the figures reinforce the iconography of George III as a Roman emperor.

POLAR BEAR

VESSEL: HMS *RESOLUTE*	
DATE OF VESSEL: 1850	
VESSEL TYPE: EXPLORATION SHIP	
FIGUREHEAD HEIGHT: 0.6 M	

BOUGHT FROM THE merchant marine, the *Resolute* was converted to an exploration ship to look for Sir John Franklin's missing 1845 Arctic expedition. The polar bear figurehead was, at some point, painted white, but is now worn and discoloured. It appears to be inspired by an illustration in Sir John Ross's published account of his 1818 Arctic expedition, which shows the bear's head in the same pose. When *Resolute* was broken up in 1879, a desk was made from its timbers and presented to the President of the United States. It remains in the oval office of the White House.

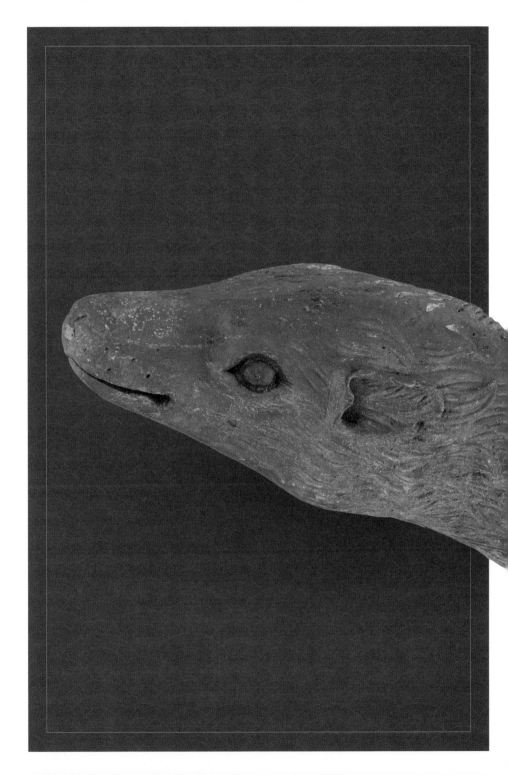

MARIANNE

VESSEL: *MARIANNE*

DATE OF VESSEL: UNKNOWN

VESSEL TYPE: MERCHANT SHIP

FIGUREHEAD HEIGHT: 1.1 M

THIS HALF-LENGTH FIGUREHEAD is thought to be from a French merchant ship. It appears to represent Marianne, the national personification of republican France. She wears a red Phrygian hat, the *bonnet rouge* or cap of Liberty, which had its origins in Roman history, being linked to the felt hats worn by freed slaves. This symbol of liberty was adopted by French revolutionaries in 1790 as they sought to overthrow the old monarchical regime and establish France as a republic. The *bonnet rouge* remains a symbol of republicanism and of radical protest in France and elsewhere.

WILLIAM WILBERFORCE

VESSEL: *WILLIAM WILBERFORCE*	
DATE OF VESSEL: 1816	
VESSEL TYPE: BRIG-RIGGED MERCHANT SHIP	
FIGUREHEAD HEIGHT: 1.5 M	

WILLIAM WILBERFORCE (1759–33) was a good friend of William Pitt the Younger, who encouraged him to focus on the abolition of the slave trade. Along with many others, he campaigned for years against Britain's involvement in the inhuman trade, finally achieving success in 1807. Wilberforce then participated in the move to abolish slavery in the British colonies, which was achieved in 1833, a month after he died. As a prominent politician and evangelical Christian, he supported other causes like animal welfare and lifesaving at sea. Through his published works, speaking tours, portraits and prints, he was a familiar public figure.

ELIZABETH FRY

VESSEL: *ELIZABETH FRY*

DATE OF VESSEL: UNKNOWN

VESSEL TYPE: MERCHANT SHIP

FIGUREHEAD HEIGHT: 1 M

THIS FULL-LENGTH FIGUREHEAD, possibly from a wrecked schooner, has been described as representing the Quaker and reformer Elizabeth Fry (1780–1845). She was a driving force behind new legislation to make the treatment of prisoners more humane. However, this figurehead is dressed far more fashionably than the modest Quaker attire worn by Fry. Indeed, the brown jacket, skirt and simple black hat with red flower dates from a much later period. It may be that this is a late-nineteenth-century reinterpretation of the image of Fry. The closed eyes give the figurehead a pious expression, but earlier photographs show that they were painted open.

GENERAL CHARLES GORDON

VESSEL:	*GENERAL GORDON*
DATE OF VESSEL:	UNKNOWN
VESSEL TYPE:	MERCHANT SHIP
FIGUREHEAD HEIGHT:	0.8 M

THIS HALF-LENGTH BUST of General Charles Gordon (1833–85) shows him without arms. However, bolts through the shoulder suggest he probably had them and that they have since been lost. His fez reminds us that he was Governor-General of Sudan from the late 1870s to 1880. He returned to Khartoum in 1884 to defend it against the troops of the Mahdi Muhammad Ahmed. He became a national hero in Britain, withstanding the Mahdi's forces for over a year before they overran the city and killed Gordon. His death was seen as a heroic sacrifice, despite ignoring government orders to withdraw.

MEGAERA,
A GREEK FURY

VESSEL: HMS *MEGAERA*

DATE OF VESSEL: 1849

VESSEL TYPE: SECOND CLASS FRIGATE CONVERTED TO A TROOPSHIP BEFORE LAUNCH

FIGUREHEAD HEIGHT: 1.2 M

MEGAERA WAS ONE OF the Greek and Roman goddesses of vengeance and retribution (called Furies). Megaera 'the jealous one' would punish those who committed crimes, especially marital infidelity. This figurehead uses the classic symbol of the Furies, a woman with snakes in her hair. Her green peplos mantle (classical Greek body-length garment) is draped over the left shoulder, leaving the right shoulder and breast exposed.

GREEK WARRIOR

VESSEL: *THERMOPYLAE*

DATE OF VESSEL: 1891

VESSEL TYPE: PASSENGER/CARGO STEAMSHIP

FIGUREHEAD HEIGHT: 1.3 M

THERMOPYLAE WAS NAMED after a famous Greek battle against the Persians. In 480 BC, after three days of fierce fighting, a small army under the Spartan king, Leonidas, was finally defeated by a significantly larger invading Persian army of Xerxes I. The battle in later centuries came to represent the heroic and patriotic defence of the homeland against invaders and the protection of ideas of freedom over authoritarian government. The figurehead is loosely inspired by classical sculptures of warriors from ancient Greece with a plumed helmet and a cloak draped over the shoulders.

NAIAD, SEA NYMPH

VESSEL: UNKNOWN

DATE OF VESSEL: UNKNOWN

VESSEL TYPE: MERCHANT SHIP

FIGUREHEAD HEIGHT: 1.5 M

THIS FIGUREHEAD DEPICTS a young woman in scale armour and a seaweed skirt and sleeves. The seaweed replaces the stiffened leather pteruges, or armour strips, that protected the upper legs and upper arms of ancient Greek and Roman soldiers. She holds two fish in her left hand and a fishing net slung over her left shoulder. It is unclear which Greco-Roman goddess she represents, but these attributes suggest one of the many sea nymphs of ancient mythology. It may be a stern carving rather than a figurehead. If so, it provides further evidence of how decoration emphasised particular visual narratives.

JOSEPH GRIMALDI

VESSEL: HMS *CLOWN*

DATE OF VESSEL: 1856

VESSEL TYPE: WOODEN SCREW GUNBOAT

FIGUREHEAD HEIGHT: 1.6 M

WHILE THIS IS A colourful figurehead representing a clown or jester, the most noticeable aspect are the carved words: 'Here we are again'. This was the catchphrase of the famous pantomime clown and comic actor Joseph Grimaldi (1779–1837), an excellent source of inspiration for a figurehead, although it is not a likeness. Similarly, contemporary illustrations show that the current paint scheme does not match the costumes he wore on stage. The figurehead is thought to have come from HMS *Clown*, although this is based on information received when it was presented by the Admiralty in 1936 from Devonport Dockyard.

ANIMAL REPRESENTATIONS

BULLDOG

VESSEL: HMS *BULLDOG*

DATE OF VESSEL: 1845

VESSEL TYPE: WOODEN PADDLE SLOOP

FIGUREHEAD HEIGHT: 2 M

THE FIGUREHEAD CARVERS Hellyer & Son of
Portsmouth submitted a design, on which this carving
is based, to the Admiralty for the newly built wooden
paddle sloop HMS *Bulldog* (1845). The bulldog rests
its front paws on an escutcheon containing the Union
flag, clearly making it a representation of Britain. The
wide collar, with the Latin inscription *Cave Canum*
(beware the dog), may be a later addition as it does not
feature in the original drawing. However, it is entirely
in keeping for a warship built to protect British
interests around the globe. In 1865, the ship ran
aground while engaging Haitian rebels. Despite being
unable to move and lying within point-blank range
of an enemy battery, HMS *Bulldog* sank the rebel
steamer *Valorague*, blew up the powder magazine on

shore, set fire to the town and dispersed rebel riflemen before running short of ammunition. Knowing that this action had more than lived up HMS *Bulldog*'s cautionary motto, Captain Charles Wake ordered the ship to be burned rather than allow it to fall into rebel hands. The crew were rescued by an American warship

Captain Charles Wake ordered the ship to be burned rather than allow it to fall into rebel hands

and the figurehead was later recovered, keeping the name of tenacious HMS *Bulldog* alive.

The original bulldog breed was muscular, stocky and had a vice-like jaw. It had a reputation for being prepared to fight animals larger than itself. The indelible link between Britain and the bulldog is neatly illustrated by Dr Samuel Johnson's 1755 dictionary entry: 'A dog of a particular form, remarkable for his courage; he is used in baiting the bull; and this species is so peculiar to Britain, that they are said to degenerate when they are carried to other countries.'

However, the characteristics for the bulldog are similar to those of John Bull, the human personification of England, who featured in cartoons from the eighteenth century. By the mid-nineteenth century, cartoonists began bringing the two together as companions, blurring the lines between the representation of England and Britain. The British bulldog has continued to be representative of apparently traditional British characteristics: tenacity, strength and courage. During the Second World War, the projection of Winston Churchill as a symbolic British bulldog stubbornly resisting Nazi Germany is a prime example of how this continued into the twentieth century. In fact, on 8 June 1940, the *Daily Express* cartoonist Sidney Strube transplanted Churchill's head onto a bulldog, which stood astride a map of Britain defiantly looking out across the Channel as Hitler's forces began to conquer western Europe. 'Go To It', a rallying call to the British people, is painted on his tin helmet.

The use of animals to represent warships was common and can be traced back to the seventeenth century when many warships had a stylised lion figurehead.

The British bulldog has continued to be representative of apparently traditional British characteristics

These figureheads did not necessarily match the name of the ship, but were a regal symbol, connecting the monarch to the warship as a sign of their maritime power. Over time, especially into the nineteenth century, figureheads represented the name of the ship in more literal forms.

IN FOCUS
MARITIME MYTHOLOGY

SEA GODDESS

VESSEL: UNKNOWN

DATE OF VESSEL: 19TH CENTURY

VESSEL TYPE: WOODEN MERCHANT SHIP

FIGUREHEAD HEIGHT: 1.2 M

THE LINK BETWEEN mythology and the sea has an ancient pedigree. For instance, a mosaic featuring the Roman sea god Neptune (Poseidon in the Greek myths) and his wife, Amphitrite, decorates a small house preserved on the site of Herculaneum near Pompeii, the subject matter possibly linked to the owner's occupation. The maritime stories inspired by ancient Greece and Rome, such as Jason and the Argonauts and Homer's *Odyssey*, were popular subjects for Victorian artists. This figurehead has traditionally been identified as representing Amphitrite. However, it has none of the expected queenly attributes for the consort of Poseidon. She is typically depicted swathed in robes, riding a shell and attended by *hippocampi* (mythical seahorses).

Instead, the laurel leaves and berries surrounding the figurehead's upper thighs and head may represent the nymph Daphne at her moment of transformation into a laurel bush. Mocked by Apollo, Cupid fired his bow and shot him with a golden-tipped arrow. This filled Apollo with wild and uncontrollable desire. The mischievous Cupid then fired a lead-tipped arrow at Daphne, the daughter of the river god Peneus. In contrast to Apollo, she was filled with revulsion and fled. A chase ensued with Cupid intervening to allow Apollo to catch the object of his lust. At this moment Daphne called to her father who turned her into a laurel (or bay) tree to protect his daughter's chastity. She was a popular pictorial subject for artists from the fifteenth century and interest in maritime-related myths and legends became a preoccupation for the

> *The laurel leaves and berries surrounding the figurehead's upper thighs and head may represent the nymph Daphne*

mid-nineteenth-century Pre-Raphaelite Brotherhood. It has not yet been possible to link the figurehead with any known ship named Daphne or Amphitrite.

A closer look at the top of the figurehead's head reveals a circular hole, indicating there was originally an additional carved piece as part of the figure. It may explain the position of her hands and the fact the carved laurel leaves on the top are flat. Over time, pieces of a figurehead could get lost or broken and not replaced. In this case there is no evidence to say what the carved piece could have been, although it may relate to Daphne's transmogrification.

Some mythological maritime characters were incorporated into shipboard rituals and superstitions that persist today. For example, if the figurehead truly is Amphitrite then there is a clear link to the 'Crossing the Line' ceremony that takes place when a ship passes over the equator. Crewmembers that had never

Some mythological maritime characters were incorporated into shipboard rituals and superstitions that persist today

crossed the equator were called 'pollywogs' (a term for tadpoles) and went through an initiation ceremony overseen by seamen dressed as King Neptune and his queen, Amphitrite. The pollywogs were usually found guilty of numerous crimes and punished in imaginative, and at times fairly brutal, ways before being submerged in a tank of water and accepted into the 'Ancient Order of the Deep' as 'shellbacks'. This practice continues today in merchant and naval ships, and even on some cruise ships, with the participants getting a certificate confirming their rite of passage.

UNKNOWN FEMALE FIGURE

VESSEL: *SPRING*

DATE OF VESSEL: 1867

VESSEL TYPE: MERCHANT SHIP

FIGUREHEAD HEIGHT: 0.8 M

THIS FIGUREHEAD OF A young woman in a red and white dress was either the original for the fruit-trading vessel *Spring*, or a replacement made after the ship was refitted and renamed *Gravesend* in 1892. Regardless, it is most likely an example of a generic figurehead, having no obvious iconography to link it to either name of the schooner. It has been cut very close to the bottom of the bust, removing any scrollwork of the trail-board. Unusually for the collection the remains of the small bowsprit are in place above the figurehead.

HUNTSMAN

VESSEL: *TANTIVY*

DATE OF VESSEL: 1837

VESSEL TYPE: SCHOONER-RIGGED MERCHANT SHIP

FIGUREHEAD HEIGHT: 1.2 M

A TANTIVY IS THE cry used during hunting, as well as meaning a rapid gallop, both appropriate for this figurehead. It depicts a huntsman wearing a hunt-style helmet and a black-edged scarlet jacket with a white high-collared shirt tied with a black stock tie. In his white-gloved right hand is a large extended fox's tail (brush). He holds a whip and cane in his left hand and has a riding horn slung down his right side. Complying with the dress code for a 'Gentleman Member with Colours', he is also wearing white breeches and black boots with brown leather tops.

QUEEN MARIA CHRISTINA

VESSEL: *MARIA CHRISTINA*

DATE OF VESSEL: UNKNOWN

VESSEL TYPE: MERCHANT SHIP

FIGUREHEAD HEIGHT: 0.8 M

THIS SMALL FULL-LENGTH figurehead, showing a woman dressed in a green bodice and yellow skirt with a red and gold sash and lavish jewellery, is said to represent Queen Maria Christina (1626–89). Debates focused on Christina's gender from the day she was born: nurses attending her birth misidentified the infant as a boy. Raised as a prince, she was crowned King of Sweden. Christina eschewed femininity, dressing in masculine clothing. She refused to marry or produce an heir, but did, however, have a female lover, Ebba Sparre. Christina was portrayed by Greta Garbo in *Queen Christina* (1933), predominantly wearing male clothing.

WILLIAM EWART GLADSTONE

VESSEL: *GLADSTONE*

DATE OF VESSEL: UNKNOWN

VESSEL TYPE: MERCHANT SHIP

FIGUREHEAD HEIGHT: 1 M

WILLIAM GLADSTONE (1809–98) was an influential politician, whose parliamentary career lasted 60 years. Initially a Conservative, he served as a Liberal Prime Minister on four occasions. Probably loosely based on contemporary photographs, this three-quarter-length figurehead depicts Gladstone in later life with characteristic sideburns and receding hairline. He is formally attired in a high-collared white shirt, waistcoat and dark jacket. The scroll in his arms could depict any one of the acts passed during his time in office, including the Third Reform Act in 1884 which further extended voting rights as part of wider measures to reform parliamentary representation.

LION

VESSEL: UNKNOWN

DATE OF VESSEL: c.1720s

VESSEL TYPE: UNKNOWN FOURTH OR FIFTH RATE WARSHIP

FIGUREHEAD HEIGHT: 2.3 M

A STYLISED LION WAS the standard figurehead
of smaller British warships from the seventeenth
century to the mid-eighteenth century. Representing
royalty, the lion connects the monarch to the Royal
Navy and the projection of England, later Britain, as
an ambitious maritime nation. This lion, the oldest
figurehead in the Museum's collection, is resting his
front paws on the sides of an escutcheon within which
is the cross of St George. In 1846, this early style of
lion was revived as the approved figurehead deign
for the 80-gun HMS *Lion*, which was launched at
Pembroke Dockyard the following year.

BENJAMIN DISRAELI

VESSEL: *DISRAELI*

DATE OF VESSEL: UNKNOWN

VESSEL TYPE: MERCHANT SHIP

FIGUREHEAD HEIGHT: 1.2 M

BENJAMIN DISRAELI (1804–81) was a Conservative politician and favourite of Queen Victoria, who twice served as Prime Minister. He was also a successful novelist. Disraeli's politics were closely identified with the British Empire and its projected glories, although under his premiership he also instigated social reforms. The figurehead represents Disraeli as a younger man with his characteristic unruly hair and short 'goatee' beard. He is wearing a white high-collared shirt, cream waistcoat and long black jacket, all inspired by the many photographs and portraits of him. He ended his lengthy political career in the House of Lords as the Earl of Beaconsfield.

ROSE OF TORRIDGE

VESSEL: *ROSE OF TORRIDGE*
DATE OF VESSEL: UNKNOWN
VESSEL TYPE: MERCHANT SHIP
FIGUREHEAD HEIGHT: 0.8 M

THIS SMALL FEMALE half-length figurehead is from a 169-ton fruit trading vessel, built by Cocks of Bideford. It depicts Rose Salterne, a character from Charles Kingsley's novel *Westward Ho!* (1855). Set in Bideford, north Devon, during Elizabethan times, the story follows the adventures of privateer Amyas Leigh, who joins Francis Drake and Walter Raleigh in their fight against Spain. Rose, from the village of Torridge, captures Leigh's heart. But she is kidnapped by the Spanish and burnt at the stake by the Inquisition. The figurehead, in a cream dress with red collar, is attached to a stake, signifying her martyrdom.

UNKNOWN FEMALE FIGURE

VESSEL: *DUCHESSE*

DATE OF VESSEL: UNKNOWN

VESSEL TYPE: MERCHANT SHIP

FIGUREHEAD HEIGHT: 0.5 M

A HALF-LENGTH FIGUREHEAD of a woman wearing a light blue wrap over a pale pink dress. This colour scheme is not original but the result of later repainting. The figurehead is wearing a laurel wreath on her head, suggesting that she is a Greco-Roman goddess or some other mythical character. However, there is no accompanying iconography to indicate who she may have been. The wreath was usually awarded for a victory or seen as a symbol of peace. Sydney Cumbers recovered the figurehead, plus one other, from a sail loft at the Ramsgate shipyard of Beeching, Moses and Co.

HOUSEWIFE OR MAID

VESSEL: *OLD GOODY*

DATE OF VESSEL: UNKNOWN

VESSEL TYPE: MERCHANT SHIP

FIGUREHEAD HEIGHT: 1.6 M

A THREE-QUARTER-LENGTH figurehead of a woman dressed in black with a white apron. Her right hand is across her chest, partially obscured by her shawl. The name Old Goody refers to an old English form of address for a woman and was an informal, shortened version of 'goodwife'. The figurehead is reputedly from a wrecked schooner and was later mounted above the door of a butcher's shop in Faversham before being acquired by Sydney Cumbers.

KING ALFRED

VESSEL: *SOVEREIGN*

DATE OF VESSEL: UNKNOWN

VESSEL TYPE: MERCHANT SHIP

FIGUREHEAD HEIGHT: 1 M

DURING THE VICTORIAN period, there was a renewed interest in the Anglo-Saxon past. The focus was on constitutional history and constructing a pantheon of historic heroes to underpin the growing empire. While this figurehead of an Anglo-Saxon king is unidentified, King Alfred (*c*.847–899) was a particular 'hero' and regarded as the founder of the British Navy. In 897, for example, Alfred commissioned a number of ships to defend against Viking attack. A statue of him was erected at Winchester in 1899, celebrating 1000 years since his death. The plinth inscribed 'Aelfred, To the Founder of the Kingdom and Nation'.

TIPU SULTAN

VESSEL: HMS *SERINGAPATAM*

DATE OF VESSEL: 1819

VESSEL TYPE: 46-GUN FIFTH RATE FRIGATE

FIGUREHEAD HEIGHT: 1.7 M

THE FRENCH REVOLUTIONARY and Napoleonic Wars (1793–1802, 1803–1815) put a strain on British shipbuilding capacity around the country. The Royal Navy turned to dockyards in the empire and at least 15 teak-built warships were constructed in Bombay Dockyard, India. Only one survives today in Britain: HMS *Trincomalee*, launched in 1817, and now preserved at the National Museum of the Royal Navy, Hartlepool.

HMS *Seringapatam*, one of these Bombay-built ships, was named after the battle in 1799 during which Tipu Sultan (1750–99), the last ruler of Mysore, was finally defeated by the combined forces of the British East India Company and the Nizam of Hyderabad.

Tipu and his father fought a series of wars against the advancing East India Company. The figurehead is believed to represent Tipu Sultan, but the iconography is inconclusive. The figure has no military uniform and the red, white and blue decoration is more associated with Britain than Tipu's colour scheme, which was based on his tiger motif. In addition, across India, the Far East and Africa the umbrella (or parasol) was a symbol of royal power. However, as a sultan, he would have paraded under an umbrella held by an attendant rather than hold it himself. Moreover, the mythical eagle-like bird, called a 'roc', on which he sits is more closely linked to the stories of Sindbad (the Sailor) in the *Thousand and One Arabian Nights*, where it is described as 'a bird of extraordinary size'.

In this compilation of stories, Sindbad encounters the roc on his second and fifth voyages. If the figurehead is of Tipu Sultan then it may be read as an inversion of his representation that plays down his role as a military leader. To subvert the historical narrative was one way of Britain retaining control over the visual

Across India, the Far East and Africa the umbrella (or parasol) was a symbol of royal power

narrative, undermining the fact that Tipu Sultan was a formidable adversary in India, finally being killed at Seringapatam during the Fourth Anglo-Mysore war (1798–99). Nevertheless, it would be highly unusual to depict the defeated foe as the figurehead for a ship celebrating a British victory. Indeed, it is not entirely clear that this mysterious object is a figurehead at all.

The growing resurgence in interest in India and Indian art began at the turn of the nineteenth century when it increasingly began to be seen a key British possession. This started to manifest itself through decorative arts, textiles and patterns, and literature. In this context the war against Mysore, written up in 1800 by James Salmon as *A Review of the Origin, Progress and Result, of the Late Decisive War in Mysore*

> *It would be highly unusual to depict the defeated foe as the figurehead for a ship celebrating a British victory*

with Notes, brought the events in India to a wider audience. The interest in India is illustrated by the popularity of the India Museum in London, 1801–1879. The exhibits included Tipu's mechanical tiger devouring a British soldier, which is now in the V&A Museum.Regardless of who the figurehead represents, it shows the influence of Indian culture on British art and iconography.

CONSTANCE ALBERTA BRASSEY

VESSEL: *SUNBEAM*

DATE OF VESSEL: 1874

VESSEL TYPE: THREE-MASTED STEAM YACHT

FIGUREHEAD HEIGHT: 1.6 M

THIS HALF-LENGTH GILDED figurehead of a female angel, or winged cherub, with her hands crossed over her chest represents Constance Alberta Brassey, the four-year-old daughter of the Liberal politician Thomas Brassey and his wife, Annie. Constance, nicknamed 'Sunbeam', died of scarlet fever the year before the launch of the yacht they named after her. For eleven months in 1876–77, the *Sunbeam* and the Brassey family embarked on a circumnavigation of the globe, the first undertaken for pleasure. The crew of 43 included the four surviving children: Thomas (aged 14), Mabelle (aged 11), Muriel (aged 4) and Marie (aged 2). Annie (later Lady) Brassey wrote a popular account of their adventures in 1878 but never mentioned the significance of the

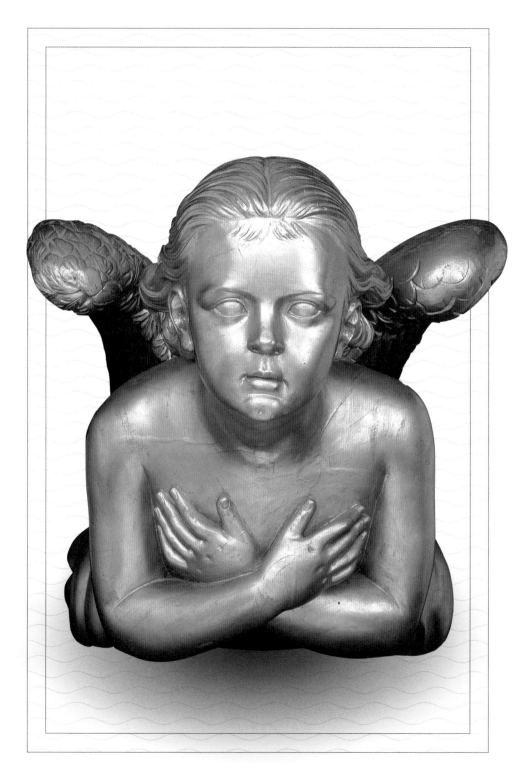

name or the figurehead. The Brasseys took *Sunbeam* on extended trips to Norway, the Mediterranean, India and Australia between 1874 and 1887 with Annie publishing further accounts of these voyages. The last volume appeared posthumously in 1889: Annie Brassey died of malarial fever in Mauritius in September 1887.

The Victorians commemorated death in many ways and it was often represented as something beautiful. In art, as well as in literature, the act of dying

Constance, nicknamed 'Sunbeam', died of scarlet fever the year before the launch of the yacht

transformed the individual into an ethereal being. Many Victorian children did not reach adulthood and parents conventionally mourned a dead child for a year. However, the memorialisation of Constance as a figurehead meant she 'accompanied' her parents on their voyages. Sentimental depictions of the death of children were popular throughout the mid-to-late-nineteenth century. For example, the death of angelic Little Nell in *The Old Curiosity Shop* traumatised Charles Dickens. He wrote to his illustrator, George Cattermole, 'I want it to express the most beautiful repose and tranquillity, and to have something of a happy look, if death can ... I am breaking my heart over this story, and cannot bear to finish it'.

Victorian-era carved headstones illustrate the symbols used to remember the dead and the cherub was a popular mode of visualising a child's soul. Moreover, these carvings could be a likeness of the dead child, forever capturing their youthfulness in stone. The figurehead of Constance extends this idea with the Brasseys preserving her likeness in the carving and her memory in the yacht's name. A photograph taken in 1873 at Niagara Falls of her older sister, Mabelle, shows similarities in the shape of the face, suggesting that she may have been the model for the figurehead.

In contrast to the elaborate figurehead, Constance's headstone at St Laurence, Catsfield, East Sussex is very simple. It records her name and dates of birth and death. Below this is the phrase 'Thy will not ours be done', a deliberate misquote from Luke 22:42 of Jesus' plea to God before Judas betrayed him. The epitaph

> *The Victorians commemorated death in many ways and it was often represented as something beautiful*

demonstrates their anguish at the loss of Constance, while recognising the piety of their beliefs. Ultimately, the survival of the figurehead at the Museum has provided Constance with a degree of perpetual commemoration that goes beyond the original intention of Annie and Thomas Brassey.

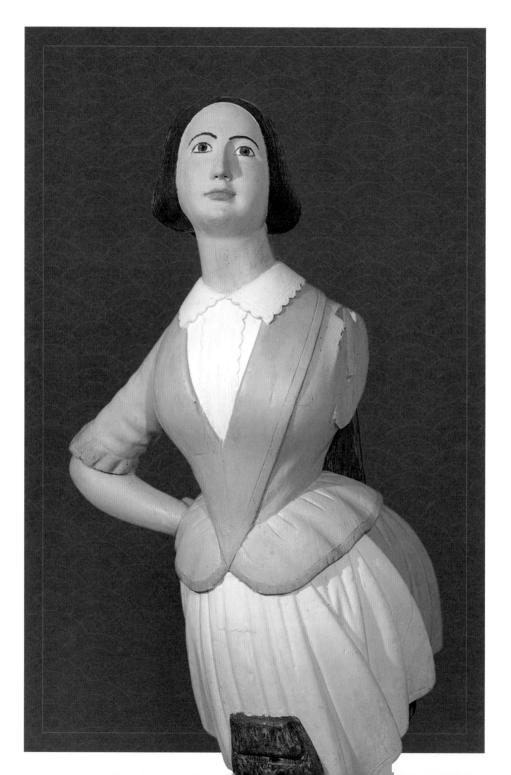

FLORENCE NIGHTINGALE

VESSEL: *FLORENCE NIGHTINGALE*

DATE OF VESSEL: UNKNOWN

VESSEL TYPE: MERCHANT SHIP

FIGUREHEAD HEIGHT: 1 M

FLORENCE NIGHTINGALE (1820–1910) came to prominence during the Crimean War (1853–56). She arrived with 38 nurses in 1854 to assist with improving conditions in the military hospitals, where deaths from disease were greater than those in battle. Her reputation spread far and wide as a result of newspaper reports on her lifesaving war work. Afterwards, she continued to pioneer sanitation and the professional training of nurses. When doing night rounds in the field hospital, Nightingale became popularly known as 'the lady with the lamp'. The figurehead's left arm is missing, but it may have held the famous lamp.

A ROMAN TRIBUNE OF THE PEOPLE

VESSEL: HMS *TRIBUNE*

DATE OF VESSEL: 1853

VESSEL TYPE: 31-GUN SECOND CLASS SCREW FRIGATE

FIGUREHEAD HEIGHT: 1.3 M

THE TRIBUNE WAS an important figure in the Roman Republic. He was the official representative elected to protect the interests of the people (the 'plebs'), usually against actions by the Senate. The figurehead, shown in classical attire, is a stylised illustration of a tribune, directly reflecting the name of the ship. However, the moustache is likely to be anachronistic as Romans in the Republican period were generally clean shaven.

SIR LANCELOT
OF THE LAKE

VESSEL: SIR *LANCELOT*

DATE OF VESSEL: 1865

VESSEL TYPE: COMPOSITE IRON AND WOODEN THREE-MASTED CLIPPER

FIGUREHEAD HEIGHT: 1.5 M

THE NINETEENTH CENTURY saw an emerging interest in medieval history and myths of King Arthur and his Knights of the Round Table. This manifested itself in art, literature and architecture from the pre-Raphaelite movement to gothic revivalism. The chivalric codes the knights abided by, as well as ideas of chastity and virtue, also struck a chord. Illustrated editions of Alfred Lord Tennyson's poems, with many inspired by Arthurian legends, were very popular and would have been freely available for carvers. Within these narratives, Lancelot took on a romantic and tragic role narrative because of his destructive love for Queen Guinevere.

N°
44

DOG

VESSEL: *SIRIUS*

DATE OF VESSEL: UNKNOWN

VESSEL TYPE: MERCHANT SHIP

FIGUREHEAD HEIGHT: 0.4 M

THIS CARVING IS THOUGHT to be a support for one of the stern quarter galleries on a merchant ship. While not a figurehead, it illustrates not only that other parts of ships had ornately carved decorations, but also that these too could relate to the ship's name. In astronomy, Sirius, known as the 'Dog Star', is the brightest star in the constellation Canis Major, or Great Dog. Because of the star's brightness, it was noticed by civilisations around the world. For instance, Polynesian voyagers used it navigate around the Pacific and for Egyptians it marked the flooding of the Nile.

DUCHESS OF SUTHERLAND

VESSEL: *DUCHESS OF SUTHERLAND*

DATE OF VESSEL: UNKNOWN

VESSEL TYPE: MERCHANT SHIP

FIGUREHEAD HEIGHT: 1.4 M

THIS FIGUREHEAD MAY have been named 'Duchess of Sunderland' by Sydney Cumbers, who believed it came from a 380-ton wood barque built in 1851 for Thomas Young by James Laing and Sons of Sunderland. The figurehead is clothed in what could be described a generic 'classical' style, wearing a cream and gold veil attached to the head with a gold tiara. She may represent Aphrodite, the Greek goddess of love, beauty and pleasure, who also had a close association with the sea. However, what is certain is that the figurehead does not depict Harriet Sutherland-Leveson-Gower, the Duchess of Sutherland (1806–68).

KING SOLOMON

VESSEL: *OPHIR*

DATE OF VESSEL: UNKNOWN

VESSEL TYPE: MERCHANT SHIP

FIGUREHEAD HEIGHT: 0.8 M

THIS HALF-LENGTH MALE figurehead is possibly from a 449-ton wooden barque built for H.H. Pettersen by Tellef Larsen at Arendal, Norway. The ship was wrecked off Worthing, East Sussex on 6 December 1896. It is believed to represent King Solomon, as suggested by the gold crown and purple tunic. In the ancient world, only kings could wear clothes dyed with expensive Tyrian purple. In the Bible, the enormously wealthy Solomon ruled over a kingdom stretching from the Euphrates to Egypt. The writer H. Rider Haggard popularised the discovery of this vast fortune in the adventure novel *King Solomon's Mines* (1885).

BERTHA MARION COGHILL

VESSEL: *BEDA* [EX *BERTHA MARION*]

DATE OF VESSEL: 1864

VESSEL TYPE: BARQUE-RIGGED MERCHANT SHIP

FIGUREHEAD HEIGHT: 2.6 M

SOME SHIPOWNERS NAMED their ships after family members, a practice that continues today. This full-length figurehead is believed to be of Bertha Marion Coghill (1863–1950), the daughter of the merchant and shipowner Harry Coghill. She was born in 1863 in Newcastle and the ship, named after her, was launched a year later. However, the carving is of a grown woman rather than an infant, raising rather obvious questions about who the figurehead depicts. It may, of course, be a generic design.

NICOLAS BOWATER

VESSEL: *NICOLAS BOWATER*

DATE OF VESSEL: 1958

VESSEL TYPE: STEAM TURBINE GENERAL CARGO SHIP

FIGUREHEAD HEIGHT: 2.4 M

THE INTRODUCTION OF iron steamships brought fundamental changes in ship design. One result of these technological developments was the disappearance of the stem-post, which meant the demise of the figurehead. Some companies kept the tradition by fixing large curved plaques to the bows instead. In this case it is a profile portrait of Nicholas Bowater (b.1943), the son of the shipowner Sir Eric Bowater, made by E.R. Bevan in 1957. It was originally painted blue but now has a bronze finish.

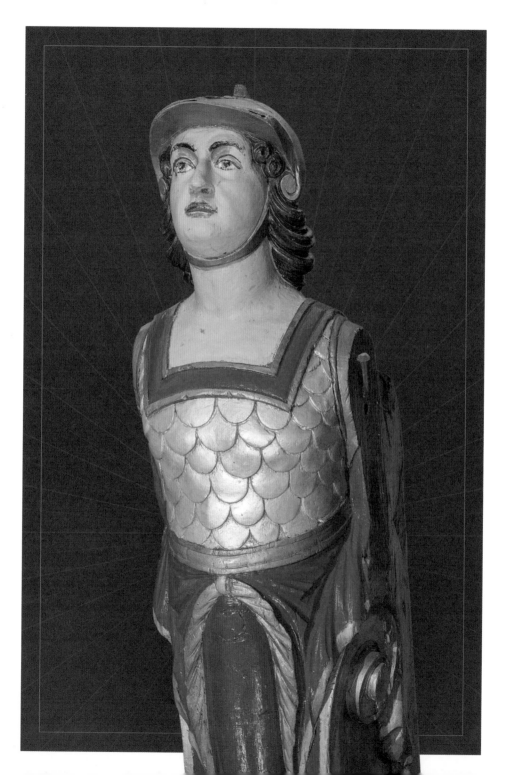

CLEOPATRA, PHARAOH OF EGYPT

VESSEL: *CLEOPATRA*

DATE OF VESSEL: UNKNOWN

VESSEL TYPE: MERCHANT SHIP

FIGUREHEAD HEIGHT: 1.7 M

THIS FIGUREHEAD IS assumed to be of Cleopatra (69–30 BCE), Egypt's last pharaoh, although the clothing does not directly support this identification. She is dressed in 'fish scale' armour more closely associated with Rome, Persia and Dacia than Egypt. The missing arms were likely to have been detachable, a reflection of its original construction. Cleopatra's relationship with Julius Caesar and her suicide following the death of her lover, Mark Anthony, have forged her tempestuous reputation. Immortalised by Shakespeare, she has been depicted in paintings, poetry, literature and on film, such as the extravagantly produced *Cleopatra* (1963) starring Elizabeth Taylor in the title role.

GENERAL COLIN CAMPBELL

VESSEL: *LORD CLYDE*

DATE OF VESSEL: 1875

VESSEL TYPE: SAILING BARQUE

FIGUREHEAD HEIGHT: 1.5 M

ORIGINALLY IDENTIFIED AS General Havelock, this figurehead is actually of General Colin Campbell, 1st Baron Clyde (1792–1862). He had an active military career, fighting in a series of conflicts in Europe and Asia, including the Crimean War and the Opium Wars. He was commander-in-chief in India during the bloodshed of the 1857–58 uprising. The figurehead, with characteristic unruly hair and prominent moustache, closely relates to the many depictions of Lord Clyde from photographs, statues and commemorative wares. The *Lord Clyde* was sold in 1902 and renamed *Trifolium*; in March 1914 it was wrecked on Gwynver Sand, near Sennen, Land's End.

1ST DUKE OF MARLBOROUGH

VESSEL: HMS *BLENHEIM*

DATE OF VESSEL: 1813–1865

VESSEL TYPE: 74 GUN THIRD RATE WARSHIP

FIGUREHEAD HEIGHT: 3 M

IT IS HIGHLY LIKELY that this large figurehead represents John Churchill, 1st Duke of Marlborough (1650–1722). He is shown anachronistically dressed in a captain's full dress uniform, 1795–1812 pattern, wearing the sash and star of the Order of the Garter, the most senior order of British chivalry. The attribution of the Duke of Marlborough is supported by the Spencer-Churchill arms on the sides of the fiddle-head scroll. The arms were granted to the family in 1733, after John's death. In design it is remarkably similar to the portrait of Captain Sir Edward Pellew by the romantic portrait painter Sir Thomas Lawrence. The carver may have drawn on this popular contemporary figure for inspiration.

While Churchill had strong naval connections (he was present at the Battle of Solebay and subsequently commissioned as a captain in James, Duke of York's Admiralty Regiment), he is best remembered as one of Britain's great generals and political leaders. Although opponents accused him of receiving preferential

Victory at the Battle of Blenheim in 1704 confirmed his status as a military genius

treatment on account of the great friendship between his wife, Sarah Churchill (1660–1744), and Queen Anne (1665–1714), victory at the Battle of Blenheim in 1704 confirmed his status as a military genius. Despite being outnumbered by the French and their Bavarian allies, the combined English and Imperial armies, led by Prince Eugene of Savoy, achieved a major victory in Germany. The French commander, Marshal Tallard, was captured and the French army lost over 34,000 men with a further 14,000 taken prisoner.

Churchill informed Sarah of his success as soon as the battle was over and in a subsequent letter declared: 'I can't end my letter without being so vain as to tell my dearest sole that within the memory of man there has been no victory so great as this.' Churchill's claims were shared by an ecstatic nation, who took to the streets to celebrate such a massive defeat of England's enemy. Contemporary reports recounted how 'Nothing was to be heard or seen in every street but the acclamation of the people, ringing of bells, bonfires firing of guns and all kinds of fireworks.' Not since the defeat of the Spanish Armada (1588) had an English victory been so complete.

Despite his undoubted charisma and diplomatic skills, Churchill had a chequered political career. In 1692 he was accused of Jacobitism and imprisoned in the Tower by order of Queen Mary. Sarah Churchill's ardent support for the Whigs and bullying behaviour eventually alienated Queen Anne, and the couple fell out of royal favour and into exile to France. The fluctuating political climate facilitated Churchill's

Not since the defeat of the Spanish Armada (1588) had an English victory been so complete

return to court and he was instrumental in the defeat of the 1715 Jacobite Rebellion. His legacy was articulated by the Duke of Wellington, who declared he could 'conceive nothing greater than Marlborough at the head of an English army'.

QUEEN CHARLOTTE

VESSEL: *ROYAL CHARLOTTE*

DATE OF VESSEL: 1824

VESSEL TYPE: ROYAL YACHT

FIGUREHEAD HEIGHT: 2.1 M

WHILE FIGUREHEADS OF ANIMALS, mythical or allegorical characters allowed carvers a certain degree of artistic licence, the subject of royalty required a greater level of accuracy. This is certainly the case with the figurehead for the royal yacht *Royal Charlotte* (1824). It is a beautifully carved and highly finished sculpture as befitted Queen Charlotte, wife of George III and mother of George IV, in whose reign the yacht was built. In fact, a Victorian display label for this figurehead described it as 'a very good likeness of Her late Majesty'.

Royal yachts were important symbols of the British monarchy's maritime credentials and often freighted with regal and national iconography. In this particular

case, the carver has decided to portray the queen early in her life after coming to Britain in 1761. The figurehead is very similar in general composition to the 1766 state portrait Queen Charlotte by Allan Ramsay, which shows her in coronation robes when she was 22 years old. Ramsay's studio produced multiple copies of this painting for other heads of state, ambassadors and institutions. It is the best-known representation of the queen, although it is not certain that this is the inspiration for the carver.

Royal yachts were important symbols of the British monarchy's maritime credentials

The three-quarter-length figurehead shows the crowned young queen in a flowing dress nipped in at the waist with a pearl encrusted belt. She holds an orb in her left hand and the sceptre in her right. The orb with a cross above it represents Christ's dominion over the Earth and therefore the monarch as God's representative on Earth. The sceptre represented the monarch's earthly power and is a symbol for good governance. Behind the figure of Queen Charlotte are two supporting cherubs, which may also represent spiritual support.

Below the dress on the left is a carved Union flag with a corresponding Hanoverian coat of arms to the right, both within shields surrounded by foliate carvings. Flowers have been intricately sculpted on the centreline where the figure slots over the (modern) supporting stem-post. The dual references to Great Britain and Hanover reflected the ancestry of George III's family, having been Electors of Hanover before his great-grandfather became King of Great Britain in 1714.

> *The dual references to Great Britain and Hanover reflected the ancestry of George III's family*

This figurehead of Queen Charlotte is more finely carved and shows much greater attention to detail than that of HMY *Royal George*, a royal yacht launched a few years earlier in 1817. This shows King George III in bust form with a laurel crown, reminiscent of Roman emperors. Figureheads of royal yachts during Queen Victoria's reign (1837–1901) were simple shields that contained coats of arms and decoration down the trail-boards. For instance, *Victoria & Albert* (1855) had two oval shields with the royal arms on the starboard side and the arms of Prince Albert on the port side, both surmounted by a crown. Even *Britannia* (1953), the last British royal yacht, had just the royal coat of arms adorning the bow – something of an understatement when compared to the *Royal Charlotte* from nearly 130 years before.

GLOSSARY

BILLET-HEAD Where the top of the stem-post has been carved with a scroll curving forwards. Sometimes it has a coat of arms or badge under the scroll.

BOW The front of a ship made up of the stem-post, trail-board and hull planking that joins to the stem-post.

BUST A carving of a person or animal that is from the head to waist without arms, usually a head-and-shoulders carving

ESCUTCHEON A shield usually with a coat of arms or emblem in the centre.

FIDDLE-HEAD Where the top of the stem-post is carved with a scroll curving backwards like the neck of a violin.

FIGUREHEAD Carved wooden sculptures that decorate the bow of sail and steam/motor ships.

FULL-LENGTH FIGUREHEAD Carving of the whole person, usually with the legs attached to the trail board.

HALF-LENGTH FIGUREHEAD A carving of a person or animal from head to waist with arms (also called a torso carving).

STEM-POST A timber curving up from the keel at the bow to which the figurehead is attached, also referred to as the cutwater.

TRAIL-BOARD A carved board either side of the stem-post, which supports the figurehead.

THREE-QUARTER-LENGTH FIGUREHEAD A carving of a person or animal from the head to above the knees.

BIBLIOGRAPHY

PRIMARY SOURCES

Navy Board and Admiralty:
Office of the Surveyor of the
Navy: In-letters Relating to Ships,
ADM 87 series, The National
Archives, Kew

SECONDARY SOURCES

Brassey, A., *A Voyage in the
'Sunbeam': Our Home on the
Ocean for Eleven Months*,
Lovell, 1881

Brewer, E.C., *Brewer's
Dictionary of Phrase & Fable*,
14th edition, Cassell, 1993

Hall, J., *Dictionary of
Subjects & Symbols in Art*,
John Murray, 1991

Hamilton, G.W., *Silent Pilots:
Figureheads in Mystic Seaport
Museum*, Mystic Seaport
Museum, 1984

Hornblower, S. & Spawforth,
A. (eds.), *The Oxford Classical
Dictionary. The Ultimate
Reference Work on the Classical
World*, 3rd edition, Oxford
University Press, 1999

Matthews, R.T., 'Britannia
and John Bull: From Birth to
Maturity', *The Historian*,
vol. 62:4, 2000

Norton, P., *Figureheads*, National
Maritime Museum, 1972

Norton, P., *Ships' Figureheads*,
David & Charles, 1976

Peters, A., *Ship decoration:
1630–1780*, Pen & Sword, 2013

Pulvertaft, D., *The Warship
Figureheads of Portsmouth*,
The History Press, 2009

Pulvertaft, D., *Figureheads
of the Royal Navy*, Seaforth
Publishing, 2011

Pulvertaft, D., 'The Colour
Schemes of British Warship
Figureheads 1727–1900',
Mariner's Mirror, vol. 104:2,
2018

Taylor, D., *Figureheads*, National
Maritime Museum, 1992

Thomas, P.N., *British
Figureheads & Ship Carvers*,
Waine Research Publications,
1995

OBJECT IDS